Contents

Acknowledgements

Our first thanks go to our assistant Jenny Sessions, who has researched and written many of the captions and helped us throughout with the text and illustrations. Toni Russell, Mary Jelfs and Rosamund Hogg have also given us a lot of help. At Broadway, the staff of Gordon Russell Limited, headed by Ray Leigh, have been very patient. We would particularly like to mention Trevor Chinn and his staff in the drawing office, Pam Edwards, Caroline Nardone, and Janet Galbraith, who brought us endless cups of tea. Adriaan Hermsen gave up much of his time to us. Douglas Barrington and his staff at the Lygon Arms, particularly Ron Wagner, have helped us in many ways. We would also like to thank the staff at The Design Council, particularly Terry Bishop. We found Paul Reilly's excellent obituary published in *The Times* on 8 October 1980 of immense value. Kate Baynes received a research grant from the Leverhulme Trust, which has given permission for us to use several fine photographs taken by Chris Ridley.

The publishers would like to thank George Allen and Unwin Ltd for permission to quote from *Designer's Trade*, and the Royal Society of Arts for permission to quote from Sir Gordon Russell's address *Skill*.

LEWIS MORLEY/TATLER

Introduction

Gordon Russell exercised an influence on every aspect of British design in the twentieth century. As an inspired administrator he made Utility furniture an exemplary model for official intervention in design standards, influenced the Festival of Britain, and shaped The Design Council into an institution that has been copied all over the world. During the 1930s, his design management of Gordon Russell Ltd, the company he founded at Broadway in Worcestershire, put it in the forefront of the small and select group of British companies that sought high standards in mass-produced goods. The radio and television cabinets made for Murphy Radio under his direction and designed by his brother Dick are international classics of modern design.

The focus of this book, however, is on the two central aspects of Gordon Russell's life. First, his work as a designer. This was concentrated in three remarkable bursts of creativity covering the initial 15 years of production at Broadway (1919 to 1934); the building of his house and garden in Gloucestershire (1925 to 1980); and a series of yew-tree pieces made in the final years of his life (1977 to 1980). Taken together they demonstrate in practical terms the working out of the second aspect: his philosophy. In this he attempted to resolve the damaging conflict that dominated modern design – the clash between hand and machine craftsmanship. Rejecting the rural Romanticism of the Arts and Crafts Movement, he was equally horrified by the total subjugation of tradition and handwork that came out of the second phase of the Bauhaus.

It is difficult for us, his daughter and son-in-law, to write an objective account of his stature as a thinker and a designer. Did he achieve what he set out to achieve? And did he set out to achieve the right thing? Other people can attempt an answer to these questions, perhaps in 20 years' time. What we can hope to provide now is something more immediate: this is an understanding of the way in which he worked and of the personality that held the philosophy and the designs together.

It is not easy to fit Gordon Russell into any accepted stereotype of the designer. To have seen him at home, up to his knees in mud excavating his garden canal next to an Irish casual labourer and an expert joiner, was to experience something almost feudal in character. In contrast, to read his comments on marketing and production methods was to recognise that a shrewd instinct for commercial success existed alongside the fundamental idealism of his approach. Then again, there is the fact that he had no formal training in design. He was, in the best sense, a practical man; his approach to design was firmly based on an understanding of materials and techniques. This helped to give his work its unique freedom from dogmatism, but it has also made him even more difficult to classify.

In fact, however, there is a tradition into which he fits perfectly: a peculiarly English one. At the start of the Industrial Revolution the course of events was dominated by a small group of manufacturers who saw clearly the links between industry and culture. Men such as Abraham Darby, Josiah Wedgwood and Matthew Boulton founded businesses that were inspired by a search for excellence as well as a capacity for making profits. These men were autocratic dynasts with a sense of purpose. They were paternalistic, but they were also passionately idealistic, forward looking and involved in public affairs. Self-made, they were seldom specialists. Against such a background, Gordon Russell's work and beliefs make sense. And, as we look to industry for a more qualitative contribution to life, they are now more topical than ever.

Ken and Kate Baynes
Stroud, Gloucestershire
October 1980

Gordon Russell as a child, photographed by his father, S.B.Russell, c1896.

Gordon's father, Sydney Bolton Russell.

Gordon's mother, Elizabeth Russell.

RUSSELL & SONS, WIMBLEDON

Chronology

1892-1919	20 May 1892	Born at Cricklewood, the eldest son of Elizabeth and Sydney Bolton Russell, who was then working in the Knightsbridge branch of the London and County Bank. After living in Tooting Bec and Repton, S.B. Russell bought the Lygon Arms hotel at Broadway.
	1 February 1904	Moved with his mother, two brothers and a nurse from Repton to join his father in Worcestershire.
	11 January 1908	After leaving the Grammar School at Chipping Campden at the end of the Christmas term 1907, sailed from Liverpool for the River Plate as purser on the *SS Veronese*, whose captain was his Uncle Joe. When he returned in April he was put in charge of the workshop where three or four men repaired old furniture, much of it for the Lygon Arms, and did a variety of other jobs. Learning from direct observation, he began to practise a number of crafts.
	22 September 1914	Joined the territorial battalion of the Worcestershire Regiment. In March 1915 was sent to France, where in January 1917 he became an officer, and described himself in his record book as 'Designer of Furniture'.
	13 February 1918	Organised a counter-attack, for which he was awarded the Military Cross.
	January 1919	Demobilised. He returned to Snowshill, where his parents had bought a house. At the age of 27 he sat on a chair in the Lygon Arms 'wondering what on earth I was going to do next'. However, this problem was solved when a few days later his brother Don, also demobilised, arrived home. Next day over a glass of port before lunch their father suggested that they join him and their mother as partners in his firm, changing the name from S.B. Russell to Russell and Sons. To provide the capital for his experiments in making new furniture, Gordon put the family antique business on its feet again. He was buyer, manager, salesman, packer, bookkeeper, transport manager, and workshop manager.

ELLIOTT & FRY

Gordon Russell (left) with his brother Don in 1917.

1920-1939	20 May 1920	On Gordon Russell's birthday Toni Denning came down from London for an interview, having applied for the job of his assistant. He later wrote in his autobiography 'she was very interested in the advertisement because it seemed an unusual job ... Poor wretch, she little dreamed of the depths of unusualness to which the job might sink.'
	21 June 1920	Toni Denning started work at Broadway (her birthday).
	November 1920	Gordon and Toni became engaged. After this Gordon designed and Edgar Turner made their marriage bed.
	8 August 1921	Married Constance Elizabeth Jane Vere (Toni), daughter of Dr and Mrs F.A.V. Denning of Sligo, by whom he had three sons and one daughter. The marriage took place at St Martin-in-the-Fields Church, London. The work of designing his own marriage bed stimulated him to produce other designs, which significantly were not matching suites but individual pieces.

The marriage bed designed by Gordon Russell in 1920 and made by Edgar Turner.

TIM QUALLINGTON/DESIGN COUNCIL

Toni Russell, Gordon's wife, with their son Oliver John, c1932.

HUGO, CHELTENHAM

1922	The first exhibition of his work was held in the art gallery at Cheltenham. Gordon Russell saw that if he was to influence the furniture trade, make an impact on his generation and expand his firm profitably he must sell his ideas and his goods. A larger workshop would be needed, and machinery would have to be used together with more sophisticated techniques of management and distribution. He had the insight to realise that it was the way the machinery was used that mattered – maximum profit by the quickest possible methods would lead only to the disillusionment of the worker and the debasement of quality and design. To be successful he must publicise and explain his controversial ideas. He started by writing a pamphlet called *Honesty and the Crafts* and general articles.
1923	Exhibited a café in the North Court of the Victoria and Albert Museum in London.
1924	Exhibited at the Palace of Arts at the British Empire Exhibition at Wembley.
1924	Cut the first sod on the site of his house, Kingcombe, in Gloucestershire.
1925	Building started at Kingcombe. This was to continue until his death. Exhibited in the British Pavilion of the Paris Exhibition – Russell and Sons awarded a gold and two silver medals.
May 1926	Moved in to Kingcombe.
4 November 1927	The Russell Worshops Ltd formed.
28 September 1929	Gordon Russell Ltd founded. In October 1929 the Wall Street Crash created panic in America and within a year had destroyed the firm's considerable American market in antiques, glass, textiles and many other products. The English market for expensive furniture, for which Gordon Russell had opened a shop in Wigmore Street, almost disappeared and 'the pall swept our little ship from stem to stern'. However, the design and making of the Murphy radio cabinets filled the gap left by the loss of the American Market and gave Gordon Russell an invaluable wider experience of the commercial world.

Over the next decade the firm expanded greatly. Dick Russell, after attending the Architectural Association's School from 1924-28, took over the drawing office from Gordon, staying there until the outbreak of war in 1939. His outlook and training proved very important for the development of the company. Many distinguished designers, who came down with him from London, provided new ideas which maintained the excellent standards of design set in the 1920s. In particular, the designing of the cabinets for Murphy Radios Ltd fundamentally influenced the thinking of the furniture trade and retailers, as well as keeping the firm in business over the hard years of depression of the 1930s. Meanwhile Gordon Russell's outside commitments steadily increased.

1939 Rejoined the Special Police.

1940-1959

October 1940	German raider dropped incendiary bomb on the barn at Broadway, destroying much furniture and 20,000 yards of fine textiles which had been brought from London for safe storage.
19 October 1940	Resigned from the managing directorship of Gordon Russell Ltd. R.H. Bee took over this job.
1940	Elected Royal Designer for Industry.
1943-47	Chairman of the Board of Trade Design Panel in charge of utility furniture.
1944	Council of Industrial Design founded. Became a member.
1945	Asked to sit on the Design Committee of the Furniture Trade Working Party which had been set up by the President of the Board of Trade. Within 24 hours of taking over as President of the Board of Trade, Sir Stafford Cripps asked S.C. Leslie, Director of the Council of Industrial Design, to stage a major exhibition of British goods. This opened in September 1946 in the Victoria and Albert Museum, London with the title 'Britain Can Make It'.

1947	Appointed Director of the Council of Industrial Design.
1947	Appointed CBE.
1951	Organised the Festival of Britain.
1952	Appointed Honorary Designer of the Royal College of Art.
1955	Created a Knight Bachelor.
26 April 1956	The Design Centre opened by the Duke of Edinburgh at 28 Haymarket, London.
1959	Appointed Senior Fellow of the Royal College of Art. Awarded Design Medal of the Society of Industrial Artists and Designers.

The Upstream section of the South Bank Exhibition, Festival of Britain, in 1951.

Gordon Russell with Frank Austin, the deputy chairman of the Utility Furniture Design Panel.

The exterior of The Design Centre for British Industries in the Haymarket, London.

1960-1980   March 1960

Founded his own design practice, working from Kingcombe.

Co-opted onto diverse boards and bodies concerned with design and production such as the Design Panel of the British Railways Board, the National Council for Diplomas in Art and Design, Morton Sundour Ltd, Edinburgh Weavers Ltd and Cockade Ltd. Indeed he was a member at one time or another of the governing body of almost every organisation concerned with the arts and design, including the Royal Society of Arts, the Design and Industries Association, the Arts Council, the British Council's Fine Arts Committee, and the Royal School of Needlework. He was given an honorary degree by Birmingham University, an honorary Fellowship by the Royal College of Art, Honorary Associateship and Honorary Fellowship by the Royal Institute of British Architects and Honorary Associateship by the Institute of Landscape Architects. He was a Member and past Master of the Faculty of Royal Designers for Industry, a past Master of the Art Workers' Guild, the first Fellow of the Society of Industrial Artists and Designers, a Vice-President of the Consumers' Association, Chairman of the original Postage Stamps Advisory Committee and a member of the Bank of England's Bank Note Design Committee. He was also first chairman of the Crafts Advisory Committee of Great Britain (now the Crafts Council).

HRH Prince Philip, President of the Royal Society of Arts, presenting the Gold Albert Medal, 23 May 1963.

1962

Awarded the Gold Albert Medal of the Royal Society of Arts 'for services to industrial design', which was presented by the Duke of Edinburgh on 23 May 1963.

May 1968

Autobiography *Designer's Trade* published by George Allen and Unwin Ltd, London.

May 1968

Death of his youngest son, Oliver John.

April 1978

Diagnosed as suffering from motor neurone disease, a progressive muscular atrophy.

1 November 1978	Delivered an address entitled *Skill* to a meeting of the Society and the Faculty of Royal Designers for Industry at the Royal Society of Arts, London.
11 July 1980	Received Honorary Doctorate of the Royal College of Art at Convocation ceremony at Kingcombe.
7 October 1980	Died at Kingcombe.
10 October 1980	Buried at St James the Great Church, Chipping Campden.

The presentation of an Honorary Doctorate of the Royal College of Art at Kingcombe, 11 July 1980.

The Broadway showrooms of Gordon Russell Ltd in 1979.

The museum containing early examples of furniture at the Gordon Russell showrooms.

CHRIS RIDLEY

Frank and Wilfred Smith working on the roof of the Wool Market in Chipping Campden High Street. Gordon Russell wrote: 'How fortunate to spend the formative years of one's life in surroundings such as these. . . . I never cease to be grateful to my unknown but deeply revered teachers, the builders of these little Cotswold towns and villages.'

ROLAND DYER

Education

It would not be correct to say that Gordon Russell was self-taught as a designer. His formal education at Chipping Campden Grammar School ignored architecture, craftsmanship and design and he never went to an art school, but his father inspired him with his own deep interest in old buildings and furniture and gave him the opportunity to work alongside joiners and cabinet-makers. Added to this was the fact that, in the first years of the twentieth century, Gloucestershire was the dynamic centre of resurgent craft activity in Britain. The place, the people and the moment combined to make possible an apprenticeship with a uniquely appropriate and rich curriculum.

These influences were not homogeneous. In some ways they were contradictory. The attempt to resolve them harmoniously was the motive for 70 years' creative work in design, manufacture, education and administration.

Gordon Russell's conviction, going back to earliest childhood memories, was a respect for craft skill. In later life, when writing his revised autobiography, which he entitled *A Designer's Education*, he could easily recall his first major experience of this magic:

One, two, three... one, two, three... At the end of the last century a small boy had stopped in a London street to watch something happening. Three burly navvies – the genuine article, not the tidied-up, suburban, pre-Raphaelite variety – were standing in a group holding heavy sledge-hammers. One bent down, placed a large steel chisel upright and tapped it gently with his hand held close to the head. When it stood of its own volition he rose and gave it a mighty blow, followed by the others – one, two, three... one, two, three... one, two, three. It was a faultless rhythmic exercise, exquisitely timed and with a ringing thud at each blow. When the chisel had sunk sufficiently, the leader tapped it on the side and a large section of the road came loose. Should I ever achieve such skill?

Here was an appreciation of the most basic kind. It grew into an admiration of know-how and a desire to understand how physical things could be achieved. Significantly, this first memory involved a skill that is seldom discussed by writers on design or craftsmanship. Gordon Russell always retained an insight into the widespread nature of skill and never wanted to see the term limited to the work of designer-craftsmen or the rural crafts. This attitude was reinforced by his very early direct experience of a workshop. From the age of 12, he was able to haunt the furniture repair shop which his father had established to serve the Lygon Arms hotel in Broadway in 1904. Home from school at weekends, he explored what had been done during the week, handled old furniture that had been taken apart, and so understood unusually well exactly how it was made and how it was put together. This understanding was provided by down-to-earth, relatively unschooled craftsmen who, nevertheless, were highly skilled.

When he was 16, he took over responsibility for the workshop and began to explore further his relationship with these men and the skill they possessed:

Jim Turner, the foreman, used to be somewhat crotchety on a morning when he had a touch of indigestion or trouble at home. He would take my rough drawing, hold it upside down and, after studying it for a second or so, would say: 'How do you expect us to make this?' All work in the shop stopped, the men obviously feeling that a little light entertainment was blowing up. I had to be careful not to tell him to hold the drawing up the other way, and then to explain exactly what I meant. Although I detested these interludes I realised afterwards how extremely valuable they were. Never since then have I consciously made a drawing unless I knew exactly how the object was going to be produced. All my drawings started from the workshop not the studio.

By 1908 items for the Lygon were made in the workshop. Among them were beds and bedside tables which already displayed many of the characteristics that became familiar in the joinery pieces of the 1920s. They were sturdy items in oak with typical 'Cotswold' details such as panelled ends with chamfers on the framing and wooden pins used in the joints. They seem almost timeless in their continuity with the mainstream of English country furniture and are still very satisfying in their reassuring solidity.

This robust workshop at Broadway must have had a very different atmosphere from those established by the members of the Guild of Handicraft in Chipping Campden. C.R. Ashbee had moved the Guild there in 1903, settling his cabinet-makers, joiners, carvers, silversmiths, jewellers, enamellers, weavers and printers in a community where native stonemasons, wallers, slaters, carpenters, basket makers, wagon builders, harness makers and blacksmiths had been at work for centuries. Gordon Russell had access to both types of shop and each had its influence on him. They embodied in real life the ideological conflict that was then raging around the importance of handwork and the role of design.

The Lygon Arms, Broadway, c1904. Gordon Russell grew up in this fine house and designed much of his early furniture for it.

During the nineteenth century industrialisation had removed the small-town craftsman from his previous position as the accepted provider of domestic furniture and equipment. This meant that in many areas of production, goods were replaced by articles made in factories and distributed nationally by rail. By 1900 it had become a commonplace of radical opinion that this development led to social and aesthetic consequences that were disastrous. Ruskin and Morris were only the best known of those who identified the connections between bad appearance, poor craftsmanship and a degraded experience of work. Some commentators regarded this problem as endemic to capitalism, others sought reform within the prevailing economic system. Whatever their views on this wider issue, the majority agreed that the rejuvenation of craftsmanship and the re-establishment of the experience this offered to the worker were the fulcrum for immediate improvement. It was this that, in their various ways, Morris, Ashbee,

Gimson and the Barnsleys were attempting and which lay behind the work of the Arts and Crafts Movement.

There was an element of Romanticism in the way the idea was carried out. Against the background of what was then the world's greatest industrial country, they rejected the use of machinery and established rural workshops where relatively expensive things were made for solid, middle-class people living off the profits of industry. Because theirs was an ideological movement rather than a response to economic opportunity, the people attracted to it were quite different from the craftsmen who had previously provided the community with the everyday necessities of life. In their hands, craftsmanship became something educational and experimental

DENNIS MOSS

A bed in oak designed by Gordon Russell for the Lygon Arms c1911.

H.J. WHITLOCK & SONS LTD

The fireplace in the Great Hall of the Lygon Arms as it appeared c1910.

rather than vocational and ordinary. It was for this reason that they insisted that the craftsman should also design everything he made, introducing a radical new element that was more pedagogical than practical. Here the movement was deliberately rejecting industry's division of labour, but it was also rejecting the previous practice of craft where tradition, pattern books and discussions with the client were the normal sources of design.

In retrospect, in his address *Skill* to the Royal Society of Arts in 1978, Gordon Russell was able to rationalise the contrasting workshop experiences of these formative years in this way:

I saw that the Arts and Crafts leaders were trying to bring designer and maker together, in itself a most worthy objective, but by insisting that the craftsman should design everything that he made they went a bit too far. I knew that many first-rate craftsmen were not highly imaginative. In any case, it became clear that the designer must have a thorough knowledge of methods of production, whether by hand or machine. Of course, some of the finest craftsmen – calligraphers like Johnston, potters like Leach, glass engravers like Whistler, and so on – carried the idea in their heads and worked it out as they went along. They did not normally have a paper design at all. And of course

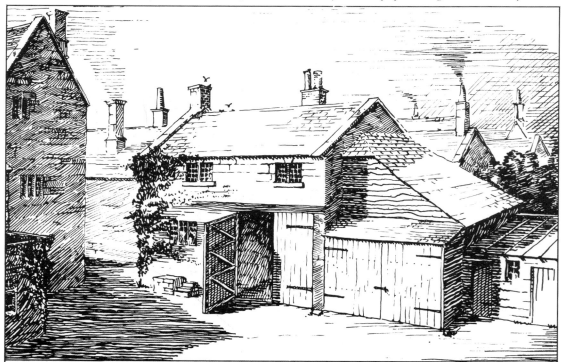

A drawing by Gordon Russell of the first workshop – a loft over the coach-house in the yard of the Lygon Arms. 1913.

there were many trades where one could not say who the designer was. The design had been gradually perfected, perhaps over centuries, which is certainly a better way of achieving a fine job than being forced to produce a new pattern every six months to please retailers. I am thinking of baskets, saddlery, footballs and many other sports goods, shoes, stone and brick walling, precision instruments, cutting and laying a hedge and so on, all of which call for a high degree of skill. Many of these most useful trades were neglected by the Arts and Crafts Movement. Can you imagine a hedger turning up at one of their meetings? Yet hedging gloves, made in Burford at one time of raw hide, *were among the finest examples of handcraft I remember.*

For all that, the Arts and Crafts Movement left a deep impression on Gordon Russell's early work, and it largely fell to people connected with it to provide his introduction to the wider horizons of design for handwork. In 1911, he established a small workshop of his own where he practised a range of crafts. A number, such as leather working, were learnt from old-established rural makers, but the majority involved self-conscious workers who naturally used the decorative style common to the years immediately before the First World War. Among the early

The second workshop at Broadway. 1907.

influences were Oliver Baker, an artist who also sold oak furniture in Stratford-upon-Avon, the Rev E.E. Dorling, who was a student of heraldry and painted the coat of arms now on the walls of the Great Hall in the Lygon Arms, and Cuthbert Wilkinson, an excellent commercial printer running the Arden Press at Letchworth. At this time, Gordon Russell made leaded lights in his workshop and designed brass and silver decorations for blackjacks which were then produced by George Hart, a silversmith and member of the Guild in Chipping Campden.

Perhaps the most fascinating item still surviving from this pre-war period is a little illuminated book of poems by Keats which he made partly to emulate his father, who was a good amateur calligrapher. It was given to the bookbinder Katherine Adams as a wedding present. She bound it in her bindery in Broadway and, on her death in 1952, it was returned by her companion, Miss Hampshire. The lettering has a confident but light touch while the decorations have exactly the period flavour that might be expected in the work of a talented student in 1914.

It is helpful to remember that the Russell family were familiar local figures, involved in a business and in local affairs in a way that brought the children into contact with an unusually diverse group of people. J.S. Sargent, Sidney Cockerell and Ernest Gimson were among significant visitors to the Lygon Arms in these years. But we can also see that once this rather shy but attractive young man showed an interest in design and craftsmanship, there were many people available who would encourage him and offer help and guidance on a more long-term basis. The thing would happen quite naturally. The particular flavour of his 'school of schools', as he called it, comes over clearly in the manuscript for his revised autobiography:

At about this time my interest in drawing led me to join a small life-class in Campden. As far as I recollect, there were about eight or nine of us. There was Paul Woodroffe, who had a stained glass studio, and J.C.M. Shepard (Shep), who worked in it, Will Hart – woodcarver, George Hart – silversmith, Alec Miller – sculptor. Fred Griggs, the etcher, turned up occasionally. I have always found discussions with people of similar interests a most valuable way of learning and it proved to be so in this case, for a number of these people remained friends of mine for many years. Sometimes I set out to walk to Campden early in the afternoon so as to have tea with one of them.

Here we catch an intimate glimpse of the world that strongly influenced the first series of designs that he produced after 1919. He always denied his

association with the Arts and Crafts Movement – and it is true that his attitude was profoundly different from theirs – but the stylistic impress of these formative years can still be seen even in the last pieces he designed in the 1970s.

Gordon Russell's enthusiasm for craftsmanship and his workshop activity before 1914 have led many people to assume that he was an expert cabinet-maker. In some instances, pieces in important collections are attributed as 'made by Gordon Russell'. This is not the case and all such attributions are incorrect. Although he was an energetic stonewaller and a robust letter cutter,

he never claimed to be anything but an amateur in any field of workmanship. What he did have was a profound understanding of the nature of craftsmanship and a sympathy for it that was rare in a designer. No doubt this was partly based on direct experience. Looking back he wrote: 'Although I did not become a skilled craftsman in these various trades I got to think from inside the materials to a considerable extent and to know the tools that were used in each of them. I was interested in the difference between joiners' chisels with wooden handles and stone masons' chisels without them, and so on. I can only claim

Two books of poetry written out by Gordon Russell between 1912 and 1914 and bound by Katherine Adams at the Eadburgha bindery in Broadway.

to have made a small bookcase in the school workshop and this proved a great trial to me as it was made of seventeenth century floor boards which had had the dust of generations of scholars ground into them.' Later he made a number of wooden handles, but that was all. His genius was to design in a way that brought out the best in the men who worked for him – challenging but never defying the inherent characteristics of the particular hand or machine skill he needed.

In addition to this ambience of craftsmanship, family interests and local surroundings provided a further well documented influence on Gordon Russell in these formative years. His father had always been interested in old buildings and it is reasonable to assume that this was one of the things that attracted him to the job of running an historic country inn. He was also an enthusiastic photographer whose subject matter ranged particularly over churches, mansions and castles. Many of his photographs survive: they are of more than amateur quality. Expeditions to take them must have brought the family into contact with a wide range of buildings and the work of developing, printing and inspecting the results would have been a good focus for discussing the qualities of architecture.

The greatest architectural influence, however, was the little town of Chipping Campden itself. This is an experience that can still be savoured. Although the High Street has been tidied up and gentrified, it remains a complete unit unbroken by any major intrusions later than the nineteenth century. Its wide, gentle curve still has the wool market built by Sir Baptist Hicks in 1627 as its fulcrum and young Gordon Russell made a sketch of this building from the window of his school dormitory when he was about 13 years old. He was fascinated by coherent, skilful and unpretentious use of stone through which generations of Cotswold masons had been able to create such a harmonious street.

Gordon Russell posing with 'some of the things I like' at Kingcombe.

SAM LAMBERT

At work on the tombstone for his father's grave at Chipping Campden.

SAM LAMBERT

On more than one occasion he said 'environment is as important as conscious training'. He frequently called for visual education to become a normal part of school work, but he was also amazed at the way in which schools could substitute second-hand for first-hand experience. Having derived his own appreciation of buildings from careful examination and enjoyment of examples near at hand, he had a keen sense of the difference between internalised understanding and the inevitably more literary perspective of books. But he meant something rather more than this: in his own experience, an appreciation of the forms of buildings was not separated from an insight into the skills and techniques necessary for making them. Not only was construction work frequently going on at the Lygon Arms, but craftsmen were always to be seen repairing, re-roofing and altering buildings in Chipping Campden. On all these activities Gordon Russell looked with sympathy and understanding: they excited him.

When he came to design and build his own house and garden in the 1920s, he deliberately tried at first to emulate the work of such craftsmen and then to extend the same principles into the use of concrete and other twentieth-century materials. Here again, he searched for a connection between hand and machine, tradition and innovation. Thus his attitude to architecture, and his contact with it, paralleled his experience of woodworking. It was a workshop style of understanding. Gordon Russell's designs for buildings exhibit exactly the same desire to extend the possibilities of craftsmanship from the 'inside' as do those for furniture.

It is less easy, at first sight, to discover the sources of his sympathy for machine craftsmanship. In his autobiography he describes the thrill of seeing one of the last of Patrick Stirling's great single-driver locomotives which were still at work when he was a child in the Midlands, and he spent hours poring over the marvellous wood engravings in his copy of *Tredgold on the Steam Engine*. A clue here is that Tredgold, in this mid-nineteenth-century book on steam-driven ships and locomotives, was celebrating quality. He was writing at a time when the divorce between industry and culture had not yet become absolute and he could still clearly see trains and ships as symbols of progress. He took it for granted that they should be finely made and well finished. Whatever its source, Gordon Russell's appreciative approach to the machine was very much based on the good example provided by engineering. It was its potential for high standards and environmental drama rather than its economic significance that he found inspiring.

In 1950 he gave a talk at the London Centre of the Institute of Industrial Administration during which he gave clear expression to these ideas:

I have always regarded the engineer as a guardian of quality. No engineer would dream of setting out to solve the problem of bridging a river or building a ship purely on the question of price. What he will do is to aim at the best solution at an economical price which is a very different matter. If he is an engineer who is also an artist he will throw a great aqueduct like the Pont de Garde across a valley and enchant travellers for centuries, or he will achieve noble viaducts in new materials like Brunel and the other early railway engineers. Or like Robert Maillart in Switzerland he will throw delicate webs of concrete across romantic gorges and leave one with the strong impression that this was the exact structure that Nature had been waiting for. The engineer's approach to the designing of woodworking machinery is entirely different from the average cabinet making firm's approach to designing furniture to be made by such machines. That is why there is still pride of craftsmanship in engineering industries. No one can take pride in shoddy workmanship, but a riveter who has done a comparatively small part of the work of building a ship usually feels a glow of pride when he sees her launched, because he knows she is well built and he has seen her grow from the day the keel was laid. His small part is therefore coherently related to the whole, and he can compare her with other ships. It is significant, as David Pye points out in his book on ships, that at a period when architecture on land was at a very low ebb, the Victorian naval architects were building the 'Cutty Sark' and other tea-clippers of astonishing beauty. You can't play the fool with ships and think of them in terms of a façade and a backside which doesn't matter!

It is clear from his writing that Gordon Russell came to believe that the machine had been monstrously misused. However, he did not believe misuse was intrinsic to it and he looked to engineering to provide the proof. In this, he echoed the German architects and designers of the Deutscher Werkbund who, in 1918, were laying the foundations of modern industrial design. Where he differed from them, was that he did not allow his appreciation to become doctrinaire or to imply the abandonment of hand craftsmanship.

If we project ourselves back to the years immediately before the First World War, we can sense that these ideas about the machine were not fully formed. The work done at this time and in the years immediately following 1919 show most strongly the influence of down-to-earth native craftsmen in the Cotswolds, the Arts and Crafts Movement and Gimson and his circle at Sapperton. It was not until these local influences had to respond to the pressures of business and the influx of new ideas in the 1920s that the possibilities of machine work could find practical expression in Gordon Russell's designs.

When he set off for the traumatic experience of trench warfare in France, Gordon Russell left behind a secure world where tradition blended happily with gentle attempts at change and reform. That world was to be shattered by social

Two towel rails designed by Gordon Russell for the Lygon Arms c1911. 'They show the development of my work. One is better than the other and has a much better finish. The rail that holds the clothes is placed diagonally and chamfers on the upright make a nice finish as an octagon at the top.'

TIM QUALLINGTON/DESIGN COUNCIL

change and economic upheaval. Nevertheless it provided a firm background. The utility of the formative years was yet to be tested, but in the event they proved to be of lasting value. They introduced the major themes that were to dominate Gordon Russell's life and work.

The Lygon Cottage showrooms, later renamed Spencer Cottage, where antiques were sold, some of which had been repaired in the Lygon workshop under the direction of the 18-year-old Gordon Russell. c1910.

Gordon Russell on the shop floor of his firm's factory at Broadway in 1959.

SAM LAMBERT

Manufacture

The 1920s and 1930s stand in an odd relationship to the present. The passage of 50 years is perhaps just the wrong amount of time to give a true perspective. The 1930s, in particular, seem both accessible and enormously remote. For the history of design they were clearly climactic, but what exactly was significant about them? Was it, for example, that the Modern Movement came to maturity in the Bauhaus and was then turned into a world-wide crusade by Hitler's persecution? Or was it, rather, that the first outlines of a new kind of mass market began to appear? Two things certainly stand out: first, a renewed popular interest in technological advance; and second, an emphasis on family life symbolised by the spread of middle-class values and an explosion of suburbia.

Perhaps 'The Thirties' exhibition at the Hayward Gallery in 1980 has helped to create the impression of a golden age for design. This is an idea that needs to be approached with caution. A distinction should be made between the normal aspect of 1930s streets, the ordinary goods in the shops, and the more extraordinary things that have been recorded in history books.

Much British design between the wars was dreadful. Frank Pick's pioneering work for London Transport, the thinking behind proposals for the Peckham Health Centre, the famous Lawn Road flats, Gropius' epoch-making school at Impington – these were the exceptions that pointed towards the future. The rule was dreary. Even the brilliant, kitsch Odeon style, which we now treasure like some faded film star, was reserved for escapist picture palaces, streamlined trains and ritzy hotels.

In furniture design, matters were at an all-time low. Never before or since have manufacturers produced so much shamelessly ill constructed work. The majority of furniture was both impractical and hideous. Machine-made, tacked-on decoration, covered in syrupy stain and varnish, served to identify period styles: Jacobean; Elizabethan; modern. It is worth making this clear, because we now identify Gordon Russell's furniture so closely with the 1920s and 1930s that his work, with that of Heal's, can begin to seem typical. In fact, it was a remarkable, almost unique, achievement, made against the general tide of manufacturing and retailing.

What exactly was this achievement? In essence, it was the creation of a company that could survive commercially without compromising its standards of aesthetics or craftsmanship. Whether or not Gordon Russell saw clearly what was ahead when he started to design and make furniture in earnest in 1919, is hard to say. What is clear is that he did not change his fundamental beliefs as the firm grew, although he had to meet a series of challenges. These included a shortage of capital; the necessity to create skilled labour; a move from hand to machine workmanship and from single-unit to mass production; launching a contract business; and opening a retail shop in London. The same period of development saw him change from designing everything made by the company to becoming its managing director and, as we would say today, its design manager. One of the distinguishing features of the enterprise in the 1930s was that it became a kind of training ground for many of the young designers and architects who were later to have a profound influence on British furniture after the Second World War.

The company's production passed through a number of well marked phases, each of which was related to a particular set of resources. Gordon Russell's first experiments took the form of two chests of drawers, each of which called for excellent dovetailing. The results were disappointing, and with characteristic realism he decided it was impossible to tackle anything of this kind until he had well trained cabinet-makers in the workshop.

He saw no reason, however, why stools and low benches, essentially joiners' work, should not be possible. So he designed a complete range of these, which were later shown in an exhibition at Cheltenham in 1922. Then, also in 1922, he again met an old acquaintance, Percy Wells, head of the cabinet-making section of the LCC Shoreditch Technical Institute. After discussion in a Lyons teashop off Old Street in the City, they decided that it would be better to repair antiques in one shop and to make furniture in another, raising the standard of finish to somewhere near that of the best hand shops. Edgar, the son of Jim Turner, accepted the company's offer of training at Shoreditch and eventually became the first skilled cabinet-maker on the staff of Russell and Sons. He quickly became a foreman, and from 1925 onwards his name began to appear on the labels of the new designs made possible by the existence of his cabinet-making skill.

It seems quite reasonable to regard the first four years from 1919 to 1923 as in some ways a tentative beginning. Gordon Russell had come out of the war with a burning desire to contribute something constructive in a world where his generation had 'destroyed so much lovely work'. He had immense respect for tradition, but he also felt that 'it was a poor age which makes no contribution of its own' and he had 'too much respect for the past not to be revolted by the regurgitations I saw on all sides'. The work produced at first owed much to the Arts and Crafts Movement in terms of style and, clearly, he was not entirely satisfied by it. A set of café furniture made in 1923 for an exhibition in the Victoria and Albert Museum is castigated in *Designer's Trade* as '(not) a bad little job, though a bit rustic and unfinished'.

We can sense gathering strength, however, and a colossal pent-up energy that was released partly by relief at the end of war and partly by his very happy marriage in 1921. These energies were

DENNIS MOSS

DENNIS MOSS

Three scenes from the Russell Workshops at Broadway, c1928. Opposite top, ladder-back chairs are having their seats rushed, while below a workman cuts tenons by machine. Above, the metalworking shop at Broadway made specially designed fittings of the required standard in small quantities. That machine and hand work should complement each other was Gordon Russell's lifelong concern.

seeking their proper outlet and were shortly to find it in four quite distinct directions.

In 1924 Gordon Russell designed an inlaid walnut cabinet which won a Gold Medal at the Paris exhibition of 1925. A fine piece, made by William Marks, it provides us with a convenient focus through which to view this new work. As we have seen, he never shared the animus against the machine which the Arts and Crafts Movement showed, but so far the scale of operations at Broadway had called only for a very limited degree of mechanisation. The furniture and metalwork now to be made would bring excellent hand and machine craftsmanship side by side with one another in the same factory. This was something quite new and it meant that Broadway was going to become the centre for design innovations as radical and influential as anything happening in the rest of Europe.

The 1925 exhibition in Paris represented the final triumph of Art Nouveau. Never quite in tune with English taste, the movement was being superseded by the complex of influences which we now recognise as 'modern design'. In retrospect, it is easy to see how contradictory the new ideas were. They had their roots in a desire to reject everything that was spurious and overblown in the Edwardian and Victorian past, but they eventually succumbed to a modernism that was equally spurious. The greatest paradox was that they combined revolutionary social idealism with a minimal understanding of popular taste or working-class culture. They embraced the machine, often for rational and realistic reasons, but sometimes simply because it was 'progressive'.

Not surprisingly, such extremism was deeply unsympathetic to Gordon Russell. His original inspiration had come from direct contact with old furniture and buildings so that he had developed a lasting respect for tradition. The tentative work he had been doing was deeply embedded in the precedents set by his immediate predeces-

sors. He might well enjoy the new, but neither background nor experience would make him want to destroy the old. It is, therefore, worthwhile to ask just what was happening when there appeared, also in 1925, a boot cupboard in Honduras mahogany that was a complete break with anything he had designed before. Superficially at least, this piece looks as deliberately and aggressively 'machine made' as anything being developed at the Bauhaus. Only the nicely displayed dovetails on the feet remain as a reminder of what had gone before.

Part of the answer can be found in the circle of friends that Gordon Russell had built up. He joined the Design and Industries Association in 1920, just when it was entering an heroic period of propaganda for the new trends that were

The boot cupboard in Honduras mahogany with brass ring handles on ebony plates, designed in 1925.

emerging on the Continent. At this time it included the majority of those who were to influence British design between the wars: Frank Pick, Allen Lane, Geoffrey Jellicoe, Ambrose Heal and many others. Then there were visits to Scandinavia and the experience of showing work in exhibitions. As early as 1923, he had begun to write the series of pamphlets and articles which continued throughout his career. It was a period of increasing involvement and self-awareness during which his horizons became international. The boot cupboard was one of the first practical expressions of these new experiences.

At a more fundamental level, the cupboard was a serious attempt to come to grips with the problems posed by mechanisation. In a characteristically cautious but forthright discussion, Gordon Russell had described his approach:

It was perhaps fifty thousand years since a man-like creature first pulled out a flint and found that he could begin to work softer materials with it. The Industrial Revolution, with intensive use of machines, was only two centuries old. Of course mistakes were being made but they could be rectified. Leadership was necessary rather than the abuse of all machines. It was the misuse of machines that struck me, and that was due to the men behind them. At least it was obvious that the machines were giving us a vast variety of things unavailable before . . .

This was guarded enthusiasm: it was balanced by scepticism and a respect for craft evolution.

Mechanisation was of more than philosophical interest. It seems likely that there were good commercial reasons for exploring the use of machinery at this stage in the company's development. Turnover was increasing, and so were the potential economies of introducing machines. But any such introduction would have a self-reinforcing effect: as machines were introduced, designs would need to respond to their capabilities and characteristics. It must have

immediately been obvious that most of the designs developed since 1919 would not work in these new circumstances; they were too closely entwined in craft traditions. Something radically different was needed if machines were to give 'a vast variety of things unavailable before' while avoiding misuse. In the circumstances it was almost inevitable that the emerging international style would provide a starting point. What is clear now, however, is that the theories of the Modern Movement were never swallowed whole at Broadway. Throughout the intensive period of innovation and experiment that was about to begin, a strong sense of tradition and an insistence on the highest possible standards of craftsmanship maintained a bedrock of common sense.

Between 1923 and 1930, therefore, four main streams of work were being made at Broadway. The first of these comprised turned chairs with rush seats of a kind derived from the work of the Herefordshire chairmaker Clisset of Bosbury and further developed by Ernest Gimson. Special versions were produced but substantial numbers of 'standard' designs were made on contract for schools and other institutions.

The second stream consisted of a huge variety of individual pieces – furniture and metalwork – mainly one-off or made in small quantities, carrying forward Arts and Crafts or Cotswold traditions in a distinctive way. Glass was also designed, but was not made, at Broadway.

Thirdly there was a small number of special pieces of furniture made to very high standards, some for individual clients, some produced as exhibition pieces like the 1925 Paris cabinet. In terms of style, there are again echoes of the Arts and Crafts Movement but these gradually vanish and a plainer presentation emerges.

Finally, the company made furniture capable of being produced in reasonable quantity using machines where appropriate and using a 'design language' clearly related to but not identical with the consciously modern furniture being designed in Europe.

Up to the early 1930s Gordon Russell designed all these items himself. The excitement of the work is caught very clearly in the carefully preserved archives of the company, which include a beautiful cabinet specially designed and made to hold the first series of drawings, and a collection of 'design books' which begin with design number one and continue through to the present day. At first the number of designs recorded is sparse, but towards the end of 1923 the entries increase, and the years 1924 and 1925 are packed with entries, mainly covering the vast number of industrial or short-run pieces.

What is evident is a practical demonstration of Gordon Russell's conviction that hand and machine craftsmanship could exist alongside one

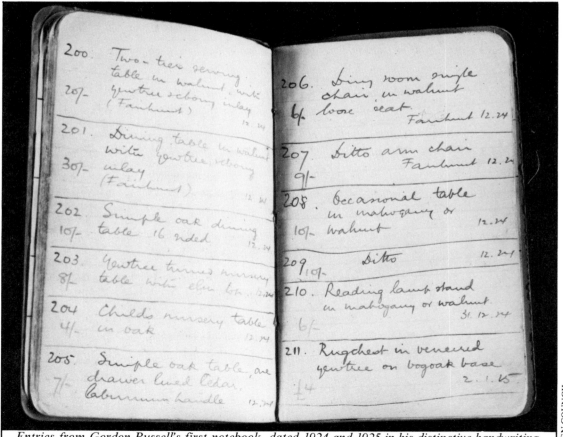

Entries from Gordon Russell's first notebook, dated 1924 and 1925 in his distinctive handwriting, give details of each individual piece made, meticulously numbered, dated and priced.

another and that both would benefit from the conjunction. The work of these years, from 1923 until he became a manager rather than a designer in the early 1930s, constitutes the foundation on which his reputation as a designer must rest. As a collection it is remarkable not only for the prolific production of individual designs, but also for the consistency with which certain themes and details recur. Many of these had roots in the formative years spent in Chipping Campden, but their synthesis into a form appropriate for machine-made furniture was a completely original contribution. It was, at the same time, a triumph to achieve this synthesis without rejecting tradition or engaging in a dehumanising celebration of everything mechanical as was happening elsewhere.

There is a further aspect to this achievement. In creating a company capable of working in this way and in providing a model of how modern furniture might be designed, he set a course which Gordon Russell Ltd was able to follow throughout the 1930s. This continuing influence, and the seminal character of Gordon Russell's designs, is well brought out by Gillian Naylor in her brief history of the company:

With the foundations so securely laid the firm then embarked on a heroic and confident period of expansion. Between 1927, when R.D. Russell returned to the firm, and the outbreak of the Second World War, output steadily increased and the design office expanded, architects, designers and practical craftsmen all contributing to the expertise. The majority of the ranges produced then were mainly for the domestic market, generally made from English timbers. The pieces were simple and unpretentious, carefully proportioned and detailed. Although semi-craft techniques were still used in the workshops throughout the 1920s many of the designs produced then could have been adapted for series production, and it is interesting to contrast the boot cupboard, with its flush doors and simple detailing, with the Gold Medal cabinet, both produced in 1925. The design of the boot cupboard was in fact remarkable for its anticipation of the furniture produced by the Russells in the 1930s, when many of the designs were inspired by a geometrical precision of form and finish, and these ranges are in themselves remarkably prophetic, for they established a vocabulary that was to be used by British furniture designers throughout the 1950s.

There is no doubt that the peak of the company's production in the 1930s occurred with the radio and television cabinets produced for Murphy and designed by R.D. Russell. Gordon Russell clearly saw them in this light and recalled how Ambrose Heal rang him up in astonishment, and with disapproval in his voice said: 'I hear you are making radio cabinets!' The reply was: 'Yes, a fascinating job. I expect it may be all that we are remembered by!' The truth is, however, that in the 1930s the company personified modern furniture and interior design in many more ways than one. As a contractor, it was the natural choice of forward-looking architects who wanted furniture or fittings made to their designs. As a retailer, it was the source of a range of furnishings and fabrics that had been carefully chosen to blend together to provide a coherent whole. As a manufacturer, it pioneered simplicity and directness in a domestic market otherwise flooded with cheap decoration and stylistic clichés.

It seems unlikely that any of this work would have been possible without the pioneering design work as its basis. The company grew from a conviction about the nature of design and it could only expand with confidence once that conviction had been put to the test and proved successful. Gordon Russell appears to have grasped this interrelationship with clarity and to have created the necessary bridge to link design and manufacture. It was done in appalling times: a triumph against all the odds.

TURNED CHAIRS WITH RUSH SEATS

Turned chairs have a special place in the history of modern English furniture, linking as they do traditional country makers with Gimson, the Barnsleys and Gordon Russell. Fortunately they are still made by Neville Neal in his workshop at Stockton near Rugby.

It was Philip Clissett, a Herefordshire chair 'bodger', who taught Gimson the art of making these chairs, and Gimson showed one that he had designed at the Arts and Crafts Society exhibition of 1890. He continued to be interested in turned chairs and encouraged Edward Gardiner to make them after he had established himself at Daneway in Gloucestershire in 1894. Such chairs were, therefore, an accepted part of the Cotswold tradition which Gimson and the Barnsleys were establishing at the turn of the century. It was logical that a workshop to make them should be set up at Broadway since they harmonise perfectly with furniture of many periods and have established themselves as 'classic' designs. Gordon Russell produced a number of variations on the basic form, some with high backs, some with arms and made of a number of different woods. In addition, more standard chairs of the same type were made in quite substantial numbers for general sale and on contract to schools, libraries and other institutions.

Turned chairs, originally made in yew with bog oak bobbins, designed by Gordon Russell in 1927 and made by the Russell Workshops Ltd, turner R.Pepper.

DENNIS MOSS

COTSWOLD DESIGNS

Writing in the excellent catalogue of work by Gimson and 'The Cotswold Group of Craftsmen' now in the collections of Leicestershire Museums, Annette Carruthers makes this comment on the way the Design and Industries Association viewed Gordon Russell's furniture:

One furniture designer who gained their approval was Gordon Russell, who set up a workshop in Broadway in 1919 where skilled craftsmen executed his ideas. Much of his early work was very close in feeling to that of Gimson and the Barnsleys and this influence continued into the 1930s when he turned to machine production, designing fine pieces for a much wider market.

In a discussion of this relationship, Gordon Russell once told the authors that it had been suggested that he might be apprenticed to Gimson immediately after the Great War. That the suggestion was not followed up seems only partly to have been the result of Gimson's death in the same year that Russell and Sons was founded. Gordon Russell certainly admired Gimson, but his own 'Cotswold' pieces are far from being copies of Gimson's. There is about them a greater feeling of robustness that seems to have come direct from the old furniture that passed through the Lygon workshops, and they are certainly less deliberately mannered.

Many of the first 'Cotswold' pieces were designed and made for the Lygon Arms to fill gaps in its seventeenth-century joinery furniture. A remarkable point is that even when, say, twenty or more mirrors were required, each was made to a separate design. This proliferation of designs was a characteristic that continued so long as hand craftsmanship was the dominant means of production, so many pieces were unique or made in very small quantities.

A sideboard made for Kingcombe in English oak with drawer sides of chestnut and handles of laburnum. Designed by Gordon Russell in 1926 and made by Russell and Sons Ltd, foreman Edgar Turner and cabinet-maker T. Allaway.

DENNIS MOSS

DENNIS MOSS

Opposite, a box mirror fitted with three drawers and ratchet adjustment (cabinet-maker T.Lees) and right, a shaving stand in walnut, both designed by Gordon Russell in 1926 and made by Russell and Sons Ltd. Above, a chest of drawers in chestnut with walnut handles. This is a panelled job with octagonal legs giving an interesting joint at the top and represents a break from the Gimson tradition of using carcasses. Russell's thinking was moving away from the Gimson approach. Gimson loved using very wide front uprights, which produced a certain amount of useless space round the corner. Russell understood why he did it: 'It looks awfully nice from the front.' Designed by Gordon Russell in 1924 and made by Russell and Sons Ltd.

Below left, a sideboard designed by Gordon Russell in 1923 and made by Russell and Sons Ltd. Below right, a wardrobe in walnut in three carcasses on a walnut base with ebony feet, designed by Gordon Russell c1927 and made by the Russell Workshops Ltd.

Opposite top, a cupboard in English walnut with bog oak handles, designed by Gordon Russell in 1926 and made by Russell and Sons Ltd. Bottom, a garden seat in oak, elm, teak or painted deal in three parts, designed by Gordon Russell in 1926 and made by Russell and Sons Ltd.

DENNIS MOSS

DENNIS MOSS

DENNIS MOSS

Gordon Russell

ABBEY STUDIOS

DENNIS MOSS

DENNIS MOSS

DENNIS MOSS

METALWORK AND GLASS

A substantial amount of metalwork was carried out at Broadway during the 1920s, much of it clearly influenced by the Arts and Crafts Movement, and in 1925 Gordon Russell designed a series of glasses which were made by Stevens and Williams.

Opposite, top left, a two-light wall sconce in polished steel and gilding metal, designed by Gordon Russell in 1925. Top right, a firescreen made of polished wrought steel, designed by Gordon Russell c1926 and made by Russell and Sons Ltd. Bottom left, a five-light sconce in silver, designed by Gordon Russell in 1924 and made by S.H.Gardiner. Bottom right, a reading lamp in copper, designed by Gordon Russell in 1924 and also made by Russell and Sons Ltd.

Below, part of a series of glass designs made in clear crystal glass using the wrythen method, in which glass is blown into a mould and then twisted so that it becomes thinner. Designed by Gordon Russell c1925 and made by Stevens and Williams.

DENNIS MOSS

FINE CABINETS

Gordon Russell always had an admiration for spectacularly fine and well made special pieces of furniture. This was to find its most complete expression in the yew-tree furniture designed and made in the last years of his life, but the process began in 1924 when two skilled cabinet-makers became available to the new company. The cabinet that was awarded a Gold Medal at the Paris Exhibition in 1925 was the first in a whole series of beautifully considered cabinets which rivalled the finest eighteenth-century work and led to other equally fine commissioned pieces.

Opposite, the cabinet awarded a Gold Medal at the Paris Exhibition of 1925, of English walnut inlaid with ebony, yew and box, with handles of ebony and laburnum and laburnum oyster inlay on interior drawer fronts. Designed by Gordon Russell in 1924 and made by Russell and Sons Ltd, cabinet-maker William Marks.

Right, a fine cabinet in bog oak, burr elm and laburnum on bog oak, designed by Gordon Russell in 1925 and made by Russell and Sons Ltd.

DENNIS MOSS

DENNIS MOSS

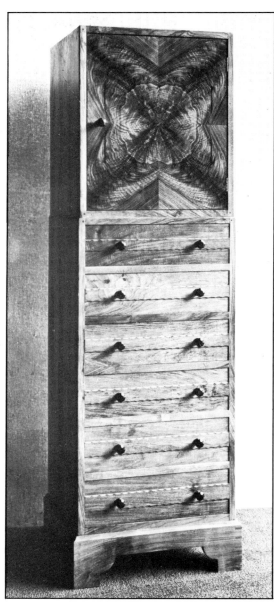

DENNIS MOSS

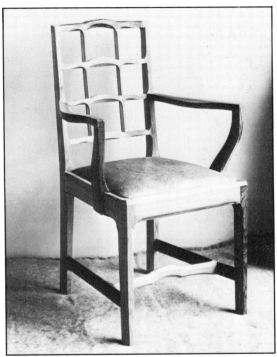

CHRIS RIDLEY

Opposite, a cupboard on a chest, in walnut lined with white mahogany and with ebony handles. Designed by Gordon Russell in 1927 and made by the Russell Workshops Ltd.

Above left, one of a set of dining-room chairs in walnut with loose seats, designed by Gordon Russell in 1924 and made by Russell and Sons Ltd. Above right, a chest of drawers made for the Rt Hon David Lloyd George from a holly tree growing in his own garden. Designed by Gordon Russell in 1928 and made by the Russell Workshops Ltd, turner R.Pepper.

THE NEW DESIGN 'LANGUAGE'

The boot cupboard, designed in 1925, was the precursor of a small number of ranges of furniture that, in the event, were to have a lasting influence on the course of furniture design in Britain. The new design 'language' appears with extraordinary confidence, as if it was already fully formed in Gordon Russell's mind. In a very short period of time, he set out the fundamentals of the road that the company was to follow up to the Second World War and, through his influence on such designers as W.H. Russell, had a substantial effect on the post-war years as well. The pattern of his thinking can be clearly seen in the wartime Utility furniture and in much of the best British work of the 1950s and 1960s. Gordon Russell described the process in his *Skill* address to the Royal Society of Arts in 1979:

We had begun to instal a few machines in order to produce in series for our shop in Broadway. This led the Arts and Crafts Society to look at us scornfully, so we were being shot at from both sides. But the fact was that we were gradually discovering what was in fairly steady demand. Our background being a small antique repair shop rather than the furniture trade, we did not think in terms of suites. And until my brother Dick, then training as an architect at the Architectural Association, was able to join us, I was under pressure designing individual pieces. Our shop at Broadway was too small an outlet to cope with a series of, say, twelve, which meant that we either had to carry too heavy a retail stock or the machines were not worth using. This quandary decided us to open a London shop, just as we ran into the depression of 1930.

Fortunately we had a chance to use our machines making radio cabinets for Murphy Radio, a lively firm which was just starting and wanted better cabinet designs than were then available. The common custom at that time was for set makers to ask woodworking firms for sketches of cabinets, from which they chose one. Without any design co-ordinator, they then bought the cloth for the aperture from a textile firm, the wave length card from a printer and the knobs from a plastics firm – knobs originally intended to pull out drawers.

So we went into mass production, occasionally 40,000 of one model. And we learned a great deal from working with engineers, who were not slow to tell us we must match up to their thousandths when we worked to crevasses such as sixteenths! We discovered that the public were greatly interested in the quality of the sets and would even accept a well designed cabinet if the set was OK. This did not happen with wardrobes, which had to be sold neat. It enabled Dick, who was by then mainly responsible for designing the cabinets, to get a clear brief – which we insisted on – from Murphy and then work out what was in our view the best design solution.

Opposite top, experiments in modular furniture photographed at Mr and Mrs S.B.Russell's house at Snowshill. Designed by Eden Minns and made by Gordon Russell Ltd in 1930. Bottom, the British Pavilion room setting at the 1937 Paris Exhibition, made by Gordon Russell Ltd.

Below, some of the cabinets designed for Murphy Radio Ltd, whose association with Gordon Russell's firm began in 1930. Designed by R.D.Russell and made by Gordon Russell Ltd.

CHRIS RIDLEY

Below left, a rustless steel-framed mirror and lamp with cast rustless steel ashtray and boxes, designed by Eden Minns c1930 and made by Gordon Russell Ltd, and right, a bookcase in rosewood veneer inlaid with ebony on a bog oak plinth with polished stainless steel door frames and cut plate-glass doors, designed by Gordon Russell in 1928 and made by Gordon Russell Ltd.

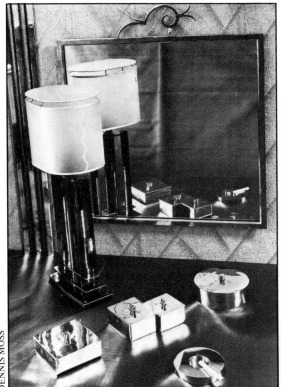

DENNIS MOSS

DENNIS MOSS

Gordon Russell's chairmanship of the Utility Furniture Design Panel marked a turning point in his career. Utility furniture first went on the market in 1943, but it is interesting to compare the dresser and chair shown here with the 'Dartington' bedroom furniture that Gordon Russell had himself designed for the Russell Workshops in 1928.

BOARD OF TRADE

DENNIS YOUNG

DENNIS MOSS

CONTRACT WORK

During the 1930s Gordon Russell Ltd became the obvious place to turn to for those architects and designers with advanced ideas who wanted furniture made to their own designs.

Below, a room setting by Gordon Russell Ltd in 1930 contains a desk in black walnut with rosewood base and sycamore lines, designed by Eden Minns; a desk chair in sycamore upholstered in natural leather, designed by R.D.Russell; a tub chair in sycamore designed by David Booth; a table lamp in natural and ebonised sycamore designed by Eden Minns; and a rug by Marian Pepler. Contract work carried out by the firm included terrace furniture for the Shakespeare Memorial Theatre at Stratford-upon-Avon, furnished throughout by Gordon Russell Ltd to the design of the architects in 1932; and Leicester City Electricity Showrooms, for which Gordon Russell Ltd supplied the furniture and carpets, also to the architects' design.

DENNIS MOSS

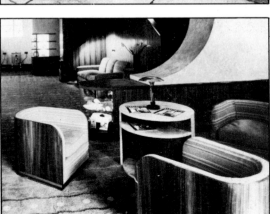

BURTON, LEICESTER

DENNIS MOSS

A box, in yew and mulberry with a laburnum base, designed by Gordon Russell and made by Adriaan Hermsen and Gordon Russell Ltd during 1978 and 1979.

Skill

An extraordinary aspect of Gordon Russell's personality during the last decade of his life, remarked on by many of the people who visited him at Kingcombe, was his continued desire to influence the future. Even during the final two years, when motor neurone disease progressively paralysed him, he continued to work on the garden and to design new pieces of furniture. When he considered rewriting his autobiography and pubishing it with the title *A Designer's Education*, his motive was to contribute to a general understanding of how designers might be formed and, therefore, the future character of the profession. To talk to him in these years was to meet with passionate conviction and a desire to see it acted on in education and practice.

In order to understand what these convictions were and to see how he imagined them becoming a reality, it is necessary to look at two closely related aspects of his work from 1970 onwards. The first was the range of yew-tree furniture which he designed. The second was the programme of writing and lectures which he carried through, culminating in the now famous talk about *Skill* for the Faculty of Royal Designers for Industry at the Royal Society of Arts on 1 November 1978. Taken together, they mark out his mature ideas on the relationship between hand and machine. They also reveal his thoughts on how to achieve quality in a world of wide but relatively thinly spread wealth.

The immediate impetus to begin designing furniture once again came directly from the need for a new dining table at Kingcombe. Getting this piece right was obviously going to be no easy matter. It had to fit harmoniously with the decorative fossil-filled floor of Derbyshire marble and existing dining chairs of English yew. This suggested that yew would be a suitable wood for the table top, but it was difficult to obtain in sufficient quantity and quality. The solution came from Chris Deane, a young tree surgeon who, in 1977, was unsuccessfully trying to save the ancient elm trees at Kingcombe. He had been contacted by the owners of a cottage; they wanted to build an extension but the ancient yew tree in their garden was in the way and would have to be felled. A timber merchant had told them that a single tree would not be commercially viable. Chris Deane, however, was not prepared to see such fine wood 'diced up into logs', feeling that it would be sacrilege to burn it as firewood. It was the biggest yew tree he had ever been asked to fell. He expressed interest, although as yet he had no outlet for the timber, and paid the owners of the cottage ten pounds for it. He had to explain that this deal was nothing to do with the company he was working for and to convince them that he was not an outright rogue.

Chris, who had his own ideas about using the tree, found a friendly saw miller who cut the wood following instructions, although he soon found problems in the form of several medieval square forged iron nails embedded in the wood.

The timber was eventually delivered to Chris and Linda Deane's garden, where it was stripped and 'cut into random chunks of six inches, four inches and two inches'. By this time Chris was wondering what he could do with the wood and so he paid a visit to Gordon Russell, saying 'I've done the most crazy thing'. Gordon Russell was very sympathetic and sent Adriaan Hermsen over to Cirencester to look at the timber. In his pocket he carried a plan, designed by Gordon Russell, of a dining table. Adriaan realised that although the wood would make a perfect top there was not enough to make the legs. He reported this back to Gordon Russell who said that he would like to come and see the wood with his wife. As soon as he saw the wood his eyes lit up and he offered to buy the lot.

The medieval nails with which the saw miller had battled also caused trouble at Broadway during the planing of the wood. However, this was not such a disadvantage in the end, because the nails had stained the wood producing beautiful plum-coloured blooms, one of the details that now give the table top its individual colour.

From the first, Gordon Russell wanted to use the opportunity of designing the table as an example of how the best hand and machine work could be combined to produce furniture of a higher quality than either could do alone. It was many years since he had designed any furniture, and while he was engaged in administrative work he had refined and developed his philosophy.

This was the moment to show decisively that the bigotry of the Arts and Crafts Movement against the machine was as damaging as the bigotry of the Bauhaus against decoration. The table and the other pieces that followed represent a practical demonstration directed against the self-destructive attitudes which he saw in some modern furniture. He was about to embark on a second astonishingly creative phase of his career as a furniture designer.

The table could not be made without a craftsman capable of working to the required standard.

The first of Gordon Russell's yew-tree pieces was this first dining table, designed in 1977. The legs are built up of laburnum, which normally does not grow to any considerable size. 'A very good job using good glues and beautifully joined.' Made by Adriaan Hermsen and Gordon Russell Ltd in 1977-78.

TIM QUALLINGTON/DESIGN COUNCIL

He also needed to be a man who could appreciate exactly what could best be made by the machines in the factory. Fortunately such a man was available – Adriaan Hermsen, who had recently retired from his job as Works Manager with the company. Hermsen had been with Gordon Russell Ltd since 1928 when, as an experienced cabinet-maker, he had come from Wells to work as charge-hand. He and Gordon Russell quickly established an unusually close working relationship. Their common background in the assumptions that inspired the enterprise at Broadway must have played a large part in this, but we can also imagine that the designer and the craftsman were both concerned to produce pieces that would be the culmination of their life's work.

The method of working was unusual and depended on the understanding between the two men. The original drawing for the table was little more than a sketch with constructional details decided during long discussions. The next stage was to set out the design to half size on large sheets of ply. At this point the general detail (such as the depth of the scallops) was approved, but one leg was made in laburnum before the finer details were agreed. Gordon Russell then did a rough drawing of the final version.

The construction of the table is very interesting – there are no rails to get in the way of a tall person's knee. To anyone accustomed to the plainness and strictly geometric forms of modern furniture the first sight of the finished table can be something of a shock. The top demonstrates a delight in the complex patterns and colour changes which the close texture of the yew produces, while the decorative laburnum base seems almost archaic in its reflection of seventeenth-century English furniture. A closer look shows that this is not in any sense a reproduction, but a genuine continuation and development of a tradition that might have been thought completely lost and even moribund.

The same characteristics can be seen in the other pieces which Gordon Russell and Hermsen produced. These include a dressing table, stool and workbox for Lady Russell, two other stools, another large table for the drawing room at Kingcombe, a clock-case, a casket and a twelve-sided occasional table. All combine hand and machine work with a decorative quality that is truly revolutionary in its implications.

Behind this highly personal work on furniture for his own house, made by a craftsman he had known for years, there was a more general idea, a more philosophical motivation. In it we can recognise a return to roots that had once again become topical. In these years, Gordon Russell believed that there was a place for small workshops alongside large manufacturing companies, not working in isolation, but rather in the closest possible collaboration. The small workshop would be able to use the sophisticated machinery whenever appropriate and it would, in its turn, feed back creative ideas and a strong sense of quality. Clearly the proposition rested on a conviction that the growing demand for quality was sufficiently widespread to make it possible for the small workshop to be economically viable in its own right. There was no suggestion that the machine work should subsidise the hand work.

In a series of tape recordings we made in 1979, we were able to explore this proposition and see how the yew-tree pieces expressed it:

'You've always been interested in the complementary use of the machine and hand work?'

'I disagreed entirely with the Arts and Crafts Movement, which felt that the machine was the very devil and wrecked everything. It wasn't the machine, it was the man behind the machine. You see, if you are making something by hand, to make it properly may take an extra hour or two. You do that because you are making the whole thing yourself and you want to be proud of it when it's finished. When you are making 10,000 of a thing,

the saving of a penny becomes of great importance and you try to save a penny . . . I prefer, instead of talking about hand and machine, to talk about quality. There are some things that can be done admirably by machine. No furniture can be made today without some machine involvement, even if it's only sawing up the wood into boards. You cannot use a pit-saw anymore: two men, one in the bottom of the pit and the other above. It is not economical and the only advantage of a pit-saw over a high-speed band mill to my mind is that with a pit-saw you can split the log in half and then have a look at it and say: "how shall we cut this up, shall we quarter it, shall we cut it into larger sections according to the tree?" With a band mill you haven't the time to stop it. The machine costs so much to run and there are so many men to attend to it and get the timber away that you have to decide before you open the thing. But, on the whole, that advantage is not so overriding that you can afford to spend twenty times as much sawing it up. The actual sawing can be done much more perfectly on the band mill.'

'We are sitting at one of the yew-tree tables you designed quite recently. How does this reflect a balance between hand and machine? How has quality been achieved?'

'You have to start with the wood itself and then see the various skills available to work it. Yew is not an easy tree to use because you seldom get any length in it and you seldom get a plank which is free of flaws. It grows in a number of different trunks which coalesce, so you get gaps in the middle of the tree; very often the tree goes hollow with age and until it is cut down you don't know what you've got. This time I was in touch with an extremely competent cabinet-maker who was very interested to pick up his box of tools again, having done an administration job for twenty years. So then we started. As you can see, the top has a very wide board in the centre. It is 16 inches wide and there are certain imperfections in the planks.'

'You've used these imperfections to very good effect haven't you?'

'Well, Adriaan Hermsen, whom I've worked with for fifty years, knows me well enough to realise what imperfections I would pass and what I would throw out. It isn't a case of throwing out everything if there's a slight imperfection. You can't do that with a wood like yew. The design had to be controlled to a considerable extent by the lengths and widths of the timber. In this table we had to put on what are called 'green ends' in old tables. They are clamped on the end of the top to hold together planks that are not thoroughly seasoned. In this case, the seasoning was very carefully controlled in a kiln. Some of these planks went into the kiln three times and there has been no movement of the six-inch-wide 'green ends' to the table. A lot of nonsense has been talked about kilning; some people say it can't make a satisfactory job. But it depends on how the thing is used. If it's not used with exactly the right heat and humidity, if it's too dry, you get the wood case-hardened and the sap can't get out. What's needed is the opposite of cooking a steak properly, there you case-harden the outside to keep the juices in!'

'You're really using the kiln as a tool aren't you?'

'Yes, but you also need a man who knows what his kiln can do and how different timbers will react. Yew is a very dense timber, it is the only English timber which will not float. Therefore, it's got to be kilned very carefully because there aren't the open grains that you get in oak and which make it much easier for the sap to escape . . . In this particular table I have used a frame of another timber altogether: laburnum. This is a wood which you can't get in very large sections. But today the glues used are far better than any that could be obtained earlier, so that I have had no compunction at all about glueing up the legs. I've been able to get a kind of leg which I think rather pleasant. I find we've gone too far in just using nothing but straight

legs in furniture. My wife has a very good pair of legs and I observed them for many years before I thought I might as well do a bit of experimenting in legs put onto furniture!'

'People may be surprised at the amount of decoration which you've introduced. It is rather startling to see so much on furniture that is being produced now.'

'I see no reason at all why one should take that easiest of all roads: no decoration at all. A number of the things I've designed use lathe shaping by hand, using square, circle and octagon together to get a good shape. I think it's about time we started thinking again over what is reasonable decoration and what isn't. The period we have gone through is really a reaction against the Victorians. Using decoration in order to prove your wealth – now this to me seems exactly like the superbly made French furniture of the eighteenth century – fine, but it was to show off what a grand chap you were. It wasn't really for use and I like things for use. I don't feel, however, that this cuts out carving, inlay or any other form of decoration that's appropriate . . . Good carving will always be costly but I don't think we should dispense with all carving just because it's going to cost a bit more. After all, why shouldn't you have just one piece of really good furniture in your house to use and look at even if it costs a bit more? People don't hesitate to apply this rule to motor cars . . .

'Presumably the kind of rather precise carving you have used is something which can be achieved to an appropriate standard today?'

'Yes, but you have got to remember that this furniture could only have happened when somebody who is interested in the history of furniture, and has handled a great deal of it over the years, meets a skilled craftsman who passionately wants to develop his skill. It couldn't be produced in large quantities: the material is not available. In any case, we shall never have a position where there will be enormous quantities of furniture produced

by hand. It will always be a limited market, but I can see a more educated public being willing to spend a bit more on a certain amount of furniture for their houses. It won't be a large public, but I think it will grow.'

'Could other people begin working in this sort of way? Could this kind of co-operation between design, industry and craftsmanship expand?'

'I'd very much like to see it expand.'

'Do you think there is anything that the industry can do to help this development along?'

'I've been very fortunate because my firm's been happy to do work in the mill. Normally a furniture firm wouldn't do this: it's just a small one-off job and a bit of a nuisance. But I think one is bound to accept the fact that if you raise the quality of handmade furniture you will in the end affect machine-made furniture. The two are interdependent. Once people start looking at furniture carefully and examining it, they become interested whether it's made by hand or machine. I would like to see more furniture that's worth looking at and I still don't see a lot of it in shop windows!'

'One ironic thing we've talked about in the past is the way some designer-craftsmen have tried to make their handmade furniture look as if it was made by machine and the way in which some machine-made furniture is made to look as if it was made by hand. What do you think about that puzzle?'

'I think one must accept that as perfectly reasonable in an age where people are standing on their heads. In any reasonable age it would seem ridiculous. There's no reason at all why, if you are making a thing by hand, it shouldn't show. Carving inlay, and other things you can do by hand, ought to look as though they've been done very skilfully by hand, not as a carving machine will do them, repeating a certain leaf every 18 inches. That kind of thing drives me round the bend!'

'Do you think we might actually be at the beginning of exciting developments? The enormous cost of labour has made many people feel that they must do most jobs around the house themselves and there's a tremendous interest in do-it-yourself and therefore increasing knowledge.'

'Yes, this is a very welcome development. It might very well lead to the next generation being far more critical than the present one. The other thing that I would like to put forward is that people should try to have one or two things in the house that are superbly made. Today you can buy very beautiful pottery that's more expensive than a cheap tea service but not extremely expensive. If you had a pottery bowl or a good piece of weaving or a well made stool or something of that sort, and you saw that every day and looked at it, your eye would become more critical of other things around. It is this comparison of a fine thing with something that isn't good enough that counts. I think you would find in the end that you would start throwing out the bad things and gradually replacing them with better things. This would be an interesting development over a period of years.'

There is in these ideas a feeling of familiarity; they seem immediately relevant to present-day conditions. Through his propaganda work at The Design Council and then the formation of the Crafts Advisory Committee, Gordon Russell himself played a large part in fostering a more general demand for quality and an interest in unique but sometimes expensive handmade things. A market now exists. In a similar way, in this era of Post-Modernism, the symbolic and psychological functions of decoration are more widely accepted and appreciated by design theorists. There is even a move to reinstate the study of traditional buildings as an aspect of architectural education. Functionalism is being relegated from its former role of revolutionary doctrine to being just another label for an historic style.

All that is true. Yet it does not have quite the right ring to it as the proper context in which to view Gordon Russell's work. Such ephemeral shifts of emphasis and the ideological debates that accompany them seem too removed from the problems of materials, skills and manufacture which, as we have seen, were always his concern.

His insistence that it was Adriaan Hermsen who made the yew-tree pieces possible is a vital clue to his attitude to design. He always worked with the production team – men, tools and machines – at his disposal while at the same time attempting to increase their capacity and skill. Although he loathed William Morris's politics and disliked many of his designs, he would have agreed with Morris in placing the nature and content of work at the centre of the industrial dilemma. In common with Morris, Gordon Russell believed that nothing could be good while work was rotten. He saw work as worthless and unsatisfying if it did not involve skill. Where he differed from Morris was in having a greater breadth of understanding in recognising skill. Morris's hatred of capitalism and capitalist industry led him to reject the skills of the industrial craftsman, but Gordon Russell saw them as important and satisfying, just as he saw in capitalist manufacturing an opportunity to create fine things.

We remember seeing him moved to tears by an account of the work of the great railway contractor Thomas Brassey. The quality of Brassey's constructions, his concern for his navvies, his respect for their skill and the affection and loyalty which they gave in return clearly seemed to him the proper basis for industrial enterprise.

He was no egalitarian: he believed that the designer and the craftsman were likely most often to be interdependent and not identical. The division of labour as such was not anathema to him. Only when it reduced men to ciphers and de-skilled their work did it become truly and wholly evil. As a successful manufacturer working in a horribly difficult market during times of depression and against a background of international unrest, he had proved to himself that quality was compatible with industry.

Yet he was aware of the fact that handwork was under enormous pressure. It is evident to us that he felt this pressure as an almost physical force: it was a palpable menace that threatened to destroy for the majority of people the experiences that he had most enjoyed in his own life. Being a realist he was fascinated, therefore, by any new pattern of working that looked to be both viable and capable of supporting fine hand craftsmanship. He saw the growth of this as essential if manufacturers and buyers were still to have available the inspiration of things done superlatively well. The yew-tree pieces were intended to be both an epitome of the quality which handwork could achieve and a demonstration of a possible relationship with public and industry.

In the closing sentence of the RSA *Skill* lecture, Gordon Russell quoted with full approval E.F. Schumacher's belief that 'the problem of production' has not yet been solved. This came after a review of his own experience and beliefs and their significance for the future which can well serve to sum up this first attempt to put his work in perspective:

I look forward to the time when every factory will have a small hand unit which would not only be valuable for making prototypes but would teach young people far more of the materials they will use than they can learn at present. Do not forget that hand and machine are complementary – an improvement in one leads in time to an improvement in the other and, as William Morris noted nearly a hundred years ago, any improvement in the work men do leads rapidly and inevitably to an improvement in the men who do it . . .

I hope I have convinced you that a somewhat different approach is needed to design in individual and quantity production. Especially, I hoped to show that hand work has not been superseded, that at its best it can give a satisfaction which a purely material approach can never give and that as we come to appreciate real values there is bound to be a considerable revival. The more things become standardised and selection therefore greatly restricted, the more there will be a demand for something different and for more humane conditions of making and selling.

TIM QUALLINGTON/DESIGN COUNCIL

The stool in the background dates from 1688. It was bought by Gordon Russell who subsequently used it as a model for the one in the front of the picture. This he called his perching stool, and in its design he explored the use of the basic octagon, square and circle. It was made by Adriaan Hermsen and Gordon Russell Ltd in 1977.

Gordon Russell

Opposite, the workbox in yew and laburnum was designed by Gordon Russell for his wife Toni in 1977. The top handles when closed form her initial, and a small slide on each side holds a glass of wine to counteract the frustrations of mending. Right, the twelve-sided table is also in yew, with shaped and carved legs and brackets, and was designed in 1979. Below, the large yew-tree table has a top for which the boards were carefully cut to form rivers of sapwood. This was Adriaan Hermsen's idea. All these pieces were made by Adriaan Hermsen, using both hand and machine methods, with the help of Gordon Russell Ltd between 1977 and 1979.

TIM QUALLINGTON/DESIGN COUNCIL

TIM QUALLINGTON/DESIGN COUNCIL

Kingcombe

Gordon and Toni Russell started their married life in Spencer Cottage, adjoining the Lygon Arms in Broadway. Until their first child Michael was born in 1922 they had no need of a garden, but when their second son Robert was born in 1924 a garden for the children became a pressing problem. After looking at a number of houses, none of which suited them, they decided to build one of their own. Toni went to look at a site which had been recommended by a local agent, thought it suitable and insisted that her husband should go over to see it. They bought the site – a field – for £60 and commissioned Leslie Mansfield to produce plans for a house, which they specified should be a solid one of local stone with internal joinery of hardwood.

Gordon Russell cut the first sod of precious topsoil on the site on Boxing Day 1924, and building began early in 1925. The Russell family moved in about May 1926, and in December their third son, Oliver, was born. They were delighted with the house, especially by the singing of the birds and the light everywhere. However, they had not considered the garden as an entity, and the first work on the garden at Kingcombe did not spring from a general master plan. This caused some difficulties later, when more land was bought on the other side of the house to make a vegetable garden and orchard, because access was difficult.

Gordon Russell, however, encouraged by his mother, soon became absorbed in the subject of garden design and in the idea of linking the house, garden and landscape into a coherent whole. He began studying gardening books, and eventually built up an extensive library. Gertrude Jekyll, William Robinson and Edith Wharton influenced him greatly, as later did Geoffrey Jellicoe, who with his partner Russell Page drew up a plan and a scheme of planting. This led to many hours of discussion, resulting in 1936 in what was then thought of as the final plan.

Throughout the 1930s both Kingcombe and its garden were the scene of feverish activity. Many trees were planted, unique fittings were designed and made at Broadway, and the foundations were laid for the extraordinary achievement which the house and garden represent today. It would be very difficult for a private enterprise today to commission work on such a scale. The death of S.B. Russell in 1938 and the outbreak of war in 1939 slowed down progress, but it never stopped, and work on Kingcombe continued right up to Gordon Russell's death in 1980. Perhaps the best way to describe what the garden meant to Gordon Russell and his wife is to use his own words to us, when we interviewed him during 1979 and asked him to tell us something about how it had been designed:

Well, I suppose it's true to say that most gardens

The drawing room at Kingcombe, with its fireplace of local Cotswold stone.

CHRIS RIDLEY

in England are designed by the owner, and few owners have much architectural or landscape training. Some are designed by architects or landscape architects, and then a landscape architect would probably make a planting plan as well and this would be carried out by nurserymen or perhaps by the owner. The garden at Kingcombe, though, was designed by somebody who started as a designer and had to learn something of horticulture as he went along. But I didn't take over plans and work to them, and except in one or two smaller cases I actually did the making as well – the planting, and a good deal of the stonework, and particularly details such as seats, benches and other things of that kind. This, I think, is rather rare – and even

rarer, it took a long time, over 50 years. Fortunately the trees were planted early on, particularly so because we have lost nearly 20 very important old elms, and good young ones coming along, but we mostly planted ash and beech, which haven't been affected.

The garden I think should be regarded as a work of art which is related to the house and to the landscape. The landscape from this site is a very beautiful one and extends nearly 14 miles, which is what the Chinese call 'borrowing one's neighbour's

view'. Obviously the plan had to take careful account of the contours on a fairly strongly sloping site, mainly to the south east. The house itself was kept very low for a number of reasons: not to obtrude on the skyline, to avoid the strong south-west wind as much as possible and to escape traffic

noise from the road, which it faces. This has become more important than it seemed at the time the house was built, when the road was only a lane, but it was widened during the war for carrying thousands of tons of stone for aerodrome building. It would have been a disaster if the house had been put higher up and nearer the road.

I think broadly I should emphasise that we like to be able to sit and have meals in the garden when we can. Shelter was therefore very important, and yew hedges were among the first things planted. We also wanted a garden where certain parts were particularly suitable for children. I am much more interested in growing flowers that like our soil, which has a good deal of lime in it, especially some of the wild ones such as primroses and the wild daffodils, which are becoming rarer and rarer elsewhere. The flowers and shrubs have to look after themselves; we can't do a great deal of transplanting in the spring. Herbaceous borders consume too much labour for us to be able to keep them up – anyway, they disappeared during the war, when we went over to food production.

The garden is not a large one – including the coppices of beech it would only be a couple of acres – but we have land around it which is let with the restriction that it is kept as pasture, so it has sheep on it from time to time which we consider a great amenity to the garden, together with our small flock of geese who delight in the pools fed by our spring and give a certain life to the garden which would be sorely missed.

I am very interested in the use of water in gardens, and I know a great many of the well known gardens in Italy and elsewhere which make splendid use of it. Obviously in England the fountains cannot have the same sparkle and feeling of coolness which is so necessary in a hot country but less welcome in an English November. On the other hand we have our pools, and I have a small canal which takes a boat for the children and is planted with water-lilies on the hot side, which is backed by *a wall partly built of bottles. I'm one of those who feel it was unfortunate when the vegetable garden was banished out of sight from the great houses of the eighteenth and ninteenth centuries. I think they are extremely interesting to look at and, as at Villendry, they can even become part of the garden itself with their formal plots of beautiful grey-green leeks and bright green cabbage and lettuce, and even dark green hedges, perhaps, of yew. At Kingcombe the vegetable garden takes up one side of the house, which is not overlooked by many windows but which can easily be seen. The south-east side is a wild garden of woodland and pools. The south-west is much more formal with a bosco of cherry trees and small enclosed space – what the Italians would call* giardino secreto *– for sitting in* shade, sun or any wind. Beyond this is a wood of beech with a good number of bluebells. On the top, north-west side there's the road and at the bottom margin the long terrace with the canal in it, forming the frame of the garden. We don't attempt to grow things like main-crop potatoes, but always some earlies, and we particularly try to have some asparagus, sea kale and globe artichokes, with plenty of peas and lettuces. We like to have chicory, and blanch it in a small bed I've made which is quite dark, next to the boiler house. This is a very satisfactory arrangement and most encouraging to peep at from above.*

Robert Micklewright's drawings of Kingcombe show, on the previous pages, the kitchen garden at the back of the house with, beside the wall, the series of arches Gordon Russell built below the garage. Above, a flight of steps towards the end of the garden is flanked by tanks full of water making a cascade in the manner of an Italian garden. Opposite, at the foot of the steps there is the canal. The bottoms of empty wine bottles, embedded in the concrete, glint in the sun and make reflections in the water. Hydrangeas are planted in large pots on top of the pillars, and Japanese flowering cherries form a bosco in which snowdrops, primroses and cyclamen bloom in the spring.

Gordon Russell

HOLLY BAKER

Bibliography

Gordon Russell was a prolific writer and speaker on design from the early 1920s onwards. The following is a selection of his more accessible books and articles.

Furniture (in the *Things We See* series). London: Penguin 1953 (revised edition).
With Jacques Groag. *The Story of Furniture*. London: Penguin 1947.
Looking at Furniture. London: Lund Humphries 1964 (revised edition).
Designer's Trade. Autobiography of Gordon Russell. London: Allen & Unwin 1968.
Skill. Address to the Royal Society of Arts and the Faculty of Royal Designers for Industry, November 1978. London: Royal Society of Arts 1978.
A Designer's Education. Unpublished autobiography of Gordon Russell's early life.
'Taste in Design' in *Art and Industry* August 1944 pp49-53.
'What is Good Design?' in *Design* 1 January 1949 pp2-6.
'The Problems of Raising Design Standards in Industry' in the *Eighth Annual Report of the Council of Industrial Design* 1952-53 (four-page insert).
'Modern Trends in Industrial Design' in *Journal of the Royal Society of Arts* vol 108 July 1960 pp565-595.

Published material on the work of Gordon Russell and Gordon Russell Limited includes the following.
'Furniture by Russell and Sons' in *Studio* vol 93 1927 p319.
Furniture designed by Gordon Russell and made by The Russell Workshops Ltd. London: Arlington Gallery 1928.
Gloag, John. 'Gordon Russell and Cotswold Craftsmanship' in *Architects Journal* 15 August 1928 pp219-226.

Boumphrey, Geoffrey. 'The Designers. 2: Gordon Russell' in *Architectural Review* vol 78 August 1935 pp77-78.
Pevsner, Nikolaus. 'Roots and Branches (Russell's development of industrial design)' in *Design* 132 December 1959 pp28-35.
Pevsner, Nikolaus. 'Patient Progress Two: Gordon Russell' in *Studies in Art, Architecture and Design volume 2: Victorian and After*. London: Thames and Hudson 1968.
Hughes-Stanton, Corin. 'Gordon Russell Today' in *Design* 233 June 1968 pp62-63.
Naylor, Gillian. *A History of Gordon Russell Limited*. Gordon Russell Limited 1976.
Woudhuysen, James. 'Beginning at the Bench' in *Design* 382 October 1980 p35.